Listening

Listening to Silence

An Anthology of
Carthusian Writings

Compiled by

Robin Bruce Lockhart

DARTON · LONGMAN + TODD

First published in 1997 by
Darton, Longman and Todd Ltd
1 Spencer Court
140–142 Wandsworth High Street
London SW18 4JJ

The right of Robin Bruce Lockhart to be identified
as the Author of this work
has been asserted in accordance with the Copyright, Designs and
Patents Act 1988

ISBN 0–232–52215–4

A catalogue record for this book is available
from the British Library

Designed by Sandie Boccacci
Phototypeset in 10½/13½ pt Raleigh by Intype London Ltd
Printed and bound in Great Britain by
Redwood Books, Trowbridge, Wiltshire

Silence

'Only silence is great; all else is weakness'
                                        Alfred de Vigny

'Elected Silence, sing to me'
                                        Gerald Manley Hopkins

'God strikes in Silence through you all'
                                        Elizabeth Browning

'My gracious Silence, Hail!'
                                        Shakespeare

'Silence is the perfectest herald of joy'
                                        Shakespeare

'Silence is deep as Eternity; speech is as shallow as Time'
                                        Carlyle

'Silence is wonderful to listen to'
                                        Hardy

'Silence is more musical than any song'
                                        Christina Rossetti

Contents

Contents

Contents

Introduction

The foundation of what was to become the Carthusian Order was laid by St Bruno in 1084. Bruno was born in Cologne in about 1030 but was a Frenchman by temperament and by upbringing, having left Cologne at an early age to study in France where he eventually took holy orders. He first gave himself to an active apostolic ministry and so impressed the Archbishop of Rheims that he was appointed Chancellor of the diocese and placed in charge of the cathedral schools. Yet, Bruno soon began to tire of the political aspects of his life and yearned for a deeper spiritual life away from the world, similar in many ways to that of the Desert Fathers.

It was in 1084 that along with six companions, Bruno, guided by divine providence and some advice from St Hugh, the Bishop of Grenoble, found a desolate deserted haven high up in the mountains beyond Grenoble where they built some log cabins and devoted themselves to a life of silent contemplation. Thus was laid the foundation of what developed into the Carthusian Order – a hermitage which was, in effect, the first Charterhouse, today known as La Grande Chartreuse. Of the Carthusian Order, Pope John XXII was to write: 'Great miracles of the world, men living in the flesh as out of the flesh . . . the greatest ornament of the Church . . . The most perfect model of a penitential and contemplative state.' Alas for Bruno, in 1090, Pope Urban II summoned him to Rome to help in the government of the Church. Bruno's yearning for the solitude of the Chartreuse in France was such that the Pope allowed him to resume it the following year but only on condition that he remained in Italy. So did Bruno found the second Charterhouse at La Torre in Calabria where he died in 1101.

Over the following centuries, Charterhouses were established throughout Europe and in the twentieth century Charterhouses have been founded across the Atlantic in the United States and in Brazil. It is the only religious Order never to have been formally reformed and of their silent solitary life in cells, Cardinal Hume has written: 'While contemplatives make up only six per cent of Holy Orders, this is the six per cent return on capital which God has reserved for himself.'

For hundreds of years within their silent enclosures Carthusians writing in their solitude alone with God have produced some of the most spiritual writing known to humankind. The mantle of spirituality of the Carthusian Order's founder, St Bruno, so profoundly evident in the little of his writings handed down to us, is readily discernible in the thoughts which have come from the pens of many subsequent Carthusians, members of an Order which has always had a spiritual force out of all proportion to the relatively small size of the Order.

Whereas St Thomas Aquinas has been termed the 'Angelic Doctor', Denys the Carthusian (1402–71), probably the most prolific of all sacred writers, is known as the 'Ecstatic Doctor'. His works, consisting of no less than forty-two volumes of some 700 pages each, deal with the widest possible range of spiritual topics, scaling the peaks of human mystical experience. Lansperge, Guiges (d. 1136), author of *Consuetudines' Cartusiae*, on which the Carthusian Statutes are based, Le Masson and Coutances are among some of the most inspiring of the many Carthusian writers. The *Life of Christ* by the Carthusian Ludoph of Saxony, the most popular religious book in the Middle Ages after Thomas à Kempis' *Imitation of Christ*, was an especial favourite of St Teresa of Avila and the same book played a large part in the conversion of the Jesuit, St Ignatius of Loyola.

Most Carthusians have written simply to marshal their own thoughts and with no intention of publishing or of writing for posterity. Although much of their work has been destroyed, fortunately a great deal has been preserved within Carthusian archives.

The disinterestedness in earthly posterity is typically evinced in the writing of the twentieth-century Carthusian, Augustin Guillerand (1877–1945), who destroyed most of his truly remarkable writings. Fortunately some survived and were edited after his death to be published in French in two short books, *Silence Cartusiene* (1950) and *Voix Cartusienne* (1953). They were subsequently translated into English and combined into one well-known book, *They Speak by Silences.*

The selection of Carthusian writings across the centuries which I have chosen for this short anthology is equally uplifting and timeless.

Carthusian spirituality has been a prime source of inspiration to many saints including the already mentioned St Teresa of Avila and St Ignatius of Loyola, but also St Dominic, St Francis Xavier and St Thomas More who tested his vocation at the London Charterhouse. It is not merely my hope but my conviction that the Carthusian spiritual message, as exemplified in this book, will prove a source of permanent inspiration to every reader – religious, priest and lay men and women.

The extracts of Carthianan writings which I have chosen for this anthology come from a great variety of sources: books, documents and letters written in a variety of languages. Much was originally written in Latin and the English versions are in many cases translations from French, Spanish and German translations from the Latin and I have had to make a number of corrections in respect of faulty translations. I am most grateful for the help I have received from a number of Charterhouses but especially that from St Hugh's Charterhouse in England with its magnificent library of some 30,000 books.

Robin Bruce Lockhart, 1997
Hove, Sussex and Collioure, France

Some Extracts from the Carthusian Statutes

Silence and Solitude

This is holy ground, where, as a man with his friend, the Lord and his servant often speak together; there, is the faithful soul frequently united to the Word of God; there, is the bride made one with her Spouse; there, earth is joined to heaven, the divine to the human. The journey, however, is long, and the way dry and barren, that must be travelled to attain the fount of water in the land of promise.

In cell the monk occupies himself usefully and in an orderly manner, reading, writing, reciting psalms, praying, meditating, contemplating, working . . . He makes a practice of resorting from time to time, to a tranquil listening of the heart, that allows God to enter through all its doors and passages.

The fruit of silence is known only to those with experience . . . there is gradually born within us of our silence itself, something that will draw us on to still greater silence . . . God has led us into solitude to speak to our heart. Let our hearts be a living altar from which there constantly ascends before God pure prayer, with which all our acts should be imbued.

Love for our brethren shows itself first of all in respect for their solitude.

By our total surrender, we profess before the world and witness to the ultimate reality of God. Our God-given joy in loving and serving him exclusively proves to the world that his gifts are a reality which can replace most of the so-called necessities of worldly life. It proves that the spiritual life is an everyday reality.

They [the Brothers] imitate the hidden life of Jesus at Nazareth when carrying out the daily tasks of the house. They praise God by their work. The Fathers, by the very fact of faithful observance of solitude, impart to the Charterhouse its special character and they give spiritual aid to the Brothers from whom in turn they receive much . . .

Whenever the Brothers are not occupied with the Divine Office in Church or with work in their Obediences, they always return to cell as to a very sure and tranquil haven. Here they remain quietly and without noise as far as possible and follow with faithfulness the Order of the day, doing everything in the presence of God and in the name of Our Lord Jesus Christ, through him giving thanks to God the Father. Here they occupy themselves usefully in reading or meditation, especially on sacred Scripture, the food of the soul, or, in the measure possible, they give themselves to prayer . . .

Some Extracts from the Carthusian Statutes

Interior recollection during work will lead a brother to contemplation. To attain this recollection it is always permissible while working to have recourse to short and, so to speak, ejaculatory prayers and even sometimes to interrupt the work with brief prayer . . .

The aim of a brother's life is above all else that he be united with Christ and that he may abide in his love. Hence, whether in the solitude of his cell or in the midst of his work, aided by the grace of his vocation, he should strive wholeheartedly and at all times to keep his mind on God.

1

St Bruno's Letters

Only two examples of Bruno having put pen to paper are extant. The first is a letter written from La Torre sometime between 1096 and 1106 to a very good friend of his, Raoul le Verd, Provost of Rheims Cathedral. Years before, Bruno and Raoul had both vowed to abandon the world for the monastic life. This Bruno had done but Raoul had failed to fulfil his vow. In this long letter, Bruno explains his love of the contemplative life. ('Only experience reveals what benefits the solitude and silence of the wilderness can bring to those who love it.')

Bruno's second letter was written in 1099 or 1100 after a visit to him in Calabria of Landwin, one of Bruno's original companions when he settled in Chartreuse; when Bruno left France for Rome, he designated Landwin as Prior of the Chartreuse community. When Landwin left Bruno to return to Chartreuse he took with him a letter from Bruno to the community at Chartreuse, which had increased in numbers since Bruno's departure. Although addressed to the whole community, at least one passage in the letter is clearly aimed at the lay Brothers.

Here are the two letters in their entirety.

Letter to Raoul le Verd, Provost of the Rheims
Chapter (written circa 1099 AD)

To the Venerable Raoul, Provost of Rheims, in a spirit of most pure charity Bruno addresses his salutations.

1. In you there shines the fidelity of our old and solid friendship, all the more remarkable and praiseworthy that it is so rare to come across among men. Despite the distances and years which have separated us, never for a moment have I felt my affection for you, old friend, wane. The great warmth of your letters reveals to me once again the tenderness of your friendship. Your many kindnesses bestowed with such prodigality upon my person and upon Brother Bernard on my behalf and also many further signs all provide further proof. My gratitude cannot reach the heights you deserve, but it gushes from a crystalline source of affection and in reply to your overwhelming kindness.

2. A traveller who on previous occasions has proved reliable left quite a long time ago as bearer of a letter from me to you: as he has never yet reappeared it seemed to me sensible to send a member of our community in order to keep you informed of what has been happening to me. As it is difficult to tell all in writing, he will be able to tell you everything in detail verbally.

3. I would like you to be aware – for perhaps it is not a question of indifference to you – that my bodily health is good (if only it were the same for the soul!). As regards external matters, all goes as well as I could wish. But in truth in my prayers I await that divine mercy which

would heal all my inner miseries and crown my inner desires.

4. I am living in Calabria with some religious brothers, a number of whom are highly cultured and who constantly keep a holy watch for the return of the Master so that they can open themselves up to him as soon as he knocks. I dwell in a wilderness well away from any dwellings of men. How can I tell you in full of its charm, its wholesome air, the vast and beautiful plain which stretches itself out between the mountain ranges, with its grassy meadows and its beflowered pastures? How can I describe the views of the hills, which slope gently all around; the shady secrets of the valleys where there is an abundance of streams, not to mention well-watered gardens and orchards planted with various trees?

5. But why do I spend my time telling you of these things? For the wise man there are other pleasures, infinitely sweeter and more valuable because of divine origin. However, when the rigour of regular discipline and spiritual exercises imposes burdens on fragile souls, the latter find relief and repose in these charms. For a bow that remains stretched too long without relaxation, loses its strength and is no longer fit for use.

6. What advantages and delights solitude and the silence of the hermitage bring to those who love it, they alone know who have experience of it. They can dwell apart and attend without interruption to the cultivation of the seeds of virtue and happily eat of the fruit of Paradise.

There alone can one actively seek a clear vision of the Heavenly Spouse, wounded by love, and behold God. There alone we are fully occupied and we grow still in that peace that the world knows not and with joy in the Holy Ghost.

Remember fair Rachel in all her elegance, she whom Jacob preferred even if she gave him fewer children than Leah. Indeed the offspring of contemplation are less numerous than those of active life; nevertheless Joseph and Benjamin were preferred by their father to their other brothers.

The better part was chosen by Mary of which she will not be deprived.

7. Think of the lovely Shunemite, the only maiden in Israel worthy to embrace to her bosom the ageing David and to restore his waning affection.

And you, my very dear brother, do you not love God above all else, so that grasped in his embrace, you are burning with a love quite divine? Then the glory of the world would fill you with disgust and you would reject the riches so overladen with cares and so burdensome; the pleasures themselves would grow repugnant, for they are no less harmful to the body than to the soul.

8. In your wisdom you will be aware of he who said, 'In he who loves the world and what is in the world, that is to say the pleasures of the flesh, the covetousness of the eyes and ambition – the love of God the Father is not to be found.' And similarly, 'He who is the friend of this world thereby becomes the enemy of God.' But then is there a worse sin or signs of a spirit out of order and in a state of collapse, an attitude more deadly or more lamentable than to rise up against him whose power is irresistible and whose justice is certain and to wish to declare war on him? Are we stronger than he is? Today his goodness ever invites us to show ourselves penitent

but does that mean to say that he will not in the end punish the insult committed by scorning this offer? What could be more contrary, more opposed to reason, to justice, to nature, than to love the creature more than the Creator, to pursue passing advantages rather than eternity itself or things terrestrial rather than celestial?

9. What are we then to do, oh my well-beloved friend? What if not to believe the divine counsels, to believe in that Truth which can never deceive? It in effect gives this advice to the world: 'Come to me, all you who are in labour, and are crushed beneath the burden and I will comfort you.' Is it not a ghastly and useless torture to be tormented by one's desires, to be constantly bruising oneself against the cares and anguish, the fear and suffering begotten by these desires? What burden is heavier than that which drags down the spirit from the summit of its sublime dignity towards the lowest depths of total wickedness? Oh my dear brother, flee away from all these troubles and anxieties and leave the tempest of this world to that harbour where there is peace and rest.

10. You well know what Wisdom has said: 'He who does not renounce all that he has cannot be my disciple.' Is it not noble, useful and pleasant to be in one's school under the teaching of the Holy Spirit, and there to learn that divine philosophy which alone bestows true happiness? Surely this is clear to all?

11. So it is therefore of the greatest importance that you examine your situation with all possible wisdom and prudence. If the love that God bestows on you seems insufficient, if the allurement of such reward does not attract you, do at least allow yourself to be convinced by the fear of inescapable punishment.

12. You know the vow which binds you, and to whom you are so bound. Omnipotent and awe-inspiring is he to whom you have made the vow to give yourself as an offering agreeable in his eyes: you have not the right to break the word you have pledged to him and it is not in your interest to do so for he cannot allow men to dishonour him with impunity.

13. You whom I love have a good memory. Remember the day we were both together with one-eyed Foulques in the little garden at Adam's house where I was then lodging. We talked of deceitful pleasures, the perishable riches of this world, and the joys of unending glory. At that moment, inflamed by divine love, we promised to make vows and we promptly decided to quit this transient life in order that we might pursue the eternal realities and to accept the habit of a monk. All this would have been done at once had not Foulques then left for Rome. We put off the execution of our plan until the time of his return. He was delayed, other forces came into play, his courage cooled off and his fervour waned.

14. What is there to be done, my very dear friend, except to discharge yourself as soon as you can of this debt? Otherwise, for so grave and so prolonged a breach of your word you will incur the wrath of the omnipotent God, and thereby terrible suffering. What great man of this world would allow any one of his subjects to cheat him of a gift he had promised to make him, especially if he attached exceptional value to it? So I do ask you to put your confidence not in my words but rather in those of the prophet and in those of the Holy Spirit. 'Make vows to the Lord your God and fulfil them, all of you who bring gifts to him who cuts short the breath of

princes and fills the kings of the earth with terror.' Listen to your God; he cuts short the breath of princes. Listen to him who fills the kings of the earth with terror. Why is the Holy Spirit so insistent about this if it is not to persuade you to fulfil the vow which you promised?

Why fulfil only with regret what will not involve you in any loss or diminution of what you have? It is you who will find therein the greater advantages and not he to whom you will be paying his dues.

15. Do not be detained by the deceitful charms of wealth so incapable of banishing unhappiness nor by the dazzle of your position as Provost which it is so difficult to perform without putting your soul in grave danger. You are established as the custodian of other men's property and not its proprietor; if you divert it to your own personal use – please do not allow my words to irritate you – it is as odious as it is unjust. If luxury and splendour allure you and you maintain a household of considerable magnificence, are you not going to be obliged to make up for the insufficiency of the income which you have earned by honest means to find methods of depriving some of what you are paying to others? To do so is neither moral nor to show oneself generous, for nothing is generous unless it is basically just.

16. I would like to see your love encompass one more thing. His Grace the Archbishop has great confidence in the advice you give and relies upon it. It is not so easy to give advice which is just and useful and the thought of the services you render to him ought not to prevent you from giving to God the tender affection which you owe him. This very tender love is so much more valuable.

Yes, all the more valuable; what is there in human

nature so deeply rooted and so deeply adapted to it as its love for goodness? And is there any being other than God himself whose goodness is comparable to his? Is there any other good apart from God himself?

What is more, in the presence of this goodness with its incomparable brilliance, splendour and beauty, the saintly soul is inflamed by the fire of love and cries out: 'With all my being I thirst for God, the omnipotent, the living God: when will I come to see the face of God himself?'

17. I hope, dear brother, that you will not disdain this friendly criticism nor turn a deaf ear to the words of the Holy Spirit. I hope, beloved friend, that you will fulfil my desire and my long waiting so that my soul be freed from the anxieties, cares and the fears it suffers on your behalf. For if it happened to you – and may God preserve you from it – that you left this life before fulfilling your vow, you would leave me prey to constant sadness, a man without the hope of any consolation.

18. That is why I am so keen that you make the point of being kind enough to come to see me when on a pilgrimage, for example, to St Nicholas. You will then meet up with the one who is more fond of you than anyone else. Together we shall then be able to discuss our affairs, the ways of our religious life and common interests. I have confidence in Our Lord that you will not regret having braved the fatigue of such a journey.

19. This letter is much longer than a normal letter: as I am not able to talk to you face to face, I have made up for this by writing more. Keep out of all danger, dear brother: don't forget my advice, and keep well. This is my most fervent wish.

I beg you to send me a copy of the life of St Remi, as it is impossible to find it down here.

Farewell.

Letter that our Venerable Father Bruno wrote in a wilderness in Calabria known as The Tower and which he addressed to his sons in Chartreuse
(written in late 1099 or early 1100)

To his sons so dearly beloved in Christ Father Bruno sends his greetings in Our Lord.

1.1. From our dear Brother Landuin's detailed account I have learned of the inflexible strictness of your wise and truly praiseworthy observance of the Rule. I have heard from him of your holy love and your untiring zeal for purity of heart, for virtue in all its forms. For all of which my soul rejoices in the Lord.

1.2. Yes, indeed I rejoice, I am led on to praise and give thanks to the Lord and yet nevertheless my sighs are of the bitterest. I rejoice to see your virtues multiplying and bearing fruit, but I suffer and blush at my own slackness and lie in the shame of my sinfulness.

1.3. So rejoice, my very dear brothers, in your happy lot and the abundance of graces which God has showered on you. Take delight also in having escaped from the tossing waves of the world and from all their dangers and shipwrecks. Take delight at having entered into a state of rest and peace and at having been able to cast anchor in the most sheltered of harbours.

1.4. Many would want to reach your goal: indeed many make every effort to attain it without ever getting there. Moreover, after having got there many are not admitted because Heaven has not granted them the grace. Also, dear brothers, you can be certain of this: anyone who has enjoyed such a wonderful form of happiness and who for one reason or another has the misfortune to lose it, will experience endless unhappiness if he has any care for the wellbeing of his soul.

2.1. As for you, my dearly beloved lay brothers, I say, 'My soul doth glorify the Lord', for I witness how his measureless mercy came to rest on you, when I hear from your Prior and most affectionate Father, how proud and happy he is on your account.

2.2. I too am full of joy to learn how in your case, who know neither how to read nor write, the omnipotent God writes with his own finger on your hearts the love and knowledge of his Holy Law. Yes, indeed, you demonstrate through your works what you love and what you know when you show generosity, truth and obedience. It is then quite evident that you know how to gather the fruit so infinitely sweet and full of life that God inscribes in your hearts.

2.3. This genuine obedience of yours is what God wants: at the same time it is a sign of complete submission to the Holy Spirit. It entails much humility and an exceptional self-surrender. It always accompanies a very pure love of the Lord and genuine charity towards our fellow men.

2.4. So, my dear brothers, remain as you are and flee as from a pest the unwholesome band of untrustworthy laymen. They distribute their writings and talk of things they do not understand and which they contradict both in their words and in their deeds. Idle beggars who wander from place to place, they belittle anyone who leads a good and religious life. They consider themselves praiseworthy if they destroy the characters of those who deserve praise, while repudiating obedience and all forms of discipline.

3.1. I wanted to keep Brother Landuin with me on account of his serious infirmities. But he feels he cannot find health, joy or life itself away from you nor anything else worthwhile, and he has not accepted my invitation. The abundant tears he has shed for you, his repeated sighs give ample proof how much you mean to him and of his flawless love he holds for all of you. And so I did not want to compel him to stay for fear of hurting him or any one of you who are so dear to me by reason of your virtue.

3.2. And so, dear brothers, I insist that you give active proof of the love you cherish in your hearts for him, your Prior and most dear Father, by giving him all the affectionate care he needs and providing him with everything that his infirmities require.

3.3. It is possible that he will refuse such loving help and that he will prefer to place his health and life at risk rather than to fail to fulfil in any way the strict observance of the Rule. Perhaps he will be ashamed if, the leader of the community, he finds himself as the least strict in this respect and afraid that if through his fault any one of you should fall into a relaxed way of life, but in my opinion there is no need to fear this.

3.4. As I have no wish to deprive you of such a grace, I authorize you to take my place so that you can oblige him to accept all you give him for his health. As for me, dear brothers, after God I have only one other desire, which is to come to see you. With the help of God, as soon as I can I will.

Adieu.

2

Twelfth and Thirteenth Centuries

St Hugh of Lincoln
(b. circa 1140; d. 1200)
entered Grande Chartreuse in 1163, Second Prior of Witham,
the first Charterhouse in England (1180–6), Bishop of Lincoln
from 1186, canonized 1220

Guiges I
Prior of the Grande Chartreuse (1109–36)

Guiges II
(d. 1188)
Ninth Prior of the Grande Chartreuse (1173–8)

Guiges du Pont
(d. 1297)

Hugh of Balma
Prior of Meyriat Charterhouse, France (1289–1304)

St Hugh of Lincoln

'Go as quickly as you can to the canons of Lincoln and tell them to make arrangements for the election of my successor, so that I too may enjoy my beloved solitude. I have lived in this stormy world for far too long and have foolishly preferred its tiresome business to the holy and delightful life which I chose from my youth.'

The kingdom of God is not restricted to monks, hermits and anchorites. When God finally judges each individual, he will not hold it against him that he has not been a hermit or a monk, but every reprobate will be rejected if he has not been a real Christian. A Christian is expected to possess three virtues; if one of them is lacking, the name of Christian without the reality will profit him nothing. For the name without the reality convicts of falsehood one who claims to follow the truth. From each will be required both truth and virtue; always to have charity in the heart, truth in the mouth and chastity in the body.

I am well aware that the church of Lincoln is obliged to serve the king in war, but only in this country; it is a fact that no service is due beyond the frontiers of England. I should therefore prefer to return to my native land and resume my normal eremitical way of life rather than remain here as bishop and cause unprecedented burdens to be laid on the church under my charge by surrendering her ancient rights.

Guiges I

One man will think another happy. I esteem him happy above all who does not strive to be lifted up with great honours in a palace, but who elects, humbly, to live like a poor countryman in a hermitage; who with thoughtful application loves to meditate in peace; who seeks to sit by himself in silence.

For to shine with honours, to be lifted up with dignities, is in my judgement a life with dangers, burdened with cares, treacherous to many and harmful to others.

With God's help, you can know what every human soul should be. But you cannot know perfectly what any soul is, not even your own. In fact, every rational soul ought to be completely devoted to God, since it is written: 'Thou shalt love the Lord thy God with thy whole heart', etc. And be kind toward your neighbour. For there follows, 'and thy neighbour as thyself'. And this is its total and sole perfection and salvation; nor should any other affection move the heart of man, except in that quasi twofold love. This must be the total and sole cause of all human actions and motions, whether spiritual or corporal, even to the least wink of the eye or movement of the finger. But who is equal to this? Yet it must be striven for. Now, these are the works of divine devotedness: contemplation, prayer, meditation, reading, the singing of psalms, performance of the sacred mysteries. The purpose of all of these is to know and love God.

Man has not been ordered to create happiness for himself, nor a god for himself but to seek a happiness which cannot be made but which is eternal. That alone can make the human mind happy and able to live, to taste, to rest, to be secure; so ensuring that it cannot lose those things. The man who lacks any of these is not happy.

The Pharisee ought not to have said: 'O God, I give thee thanks that I am not as the rest of men, as also is this publican', but, 'I am not as I am ordinarily.' For this is the speech of one who is progressing and recognizing the grace of God, while the former is the speech of a boasting fellow, and a man rashly judging about the secrets of another's heart.

God is eternal and immense. He is so great that he should be loved as much. Hence he who loves him is eternal and immense. However, no one can love him in the manner and as much as he ought to except one who knows him absolutely and perfectly, and how great he is. Yet no one can do so except he himself. Therefore true eternity and true immensity lie in him alone. God has commanded man to love that which he cannot ever love too much.

Guiges II

Reading, meditation, prayer and contemplation: these make a ladder for monks by which they are lifted up from earth to heaven. It has few rungs, yet its length is immense and wonderful, for its lower end rests upon the earth, but its top pierces the clouds and touches heavenly secrets. Just as its rungs or degrees have different names and numbers, they differ also in order and quality; and if anyone inquires carefully into their properties and functions, what each one does in relation to us, the differences between them and their order of importance, he will consider whatever trouble and care he may spend on this little and easy in comparison with the help and consolation which he gains.

Reading is the careful study of the Scriptures, concentrating all one's powers on it. Meditation is the busy application of the mind to seek with the help of one's own reason for knowledge of hidden truth. Prayer is the heart's devoted turning to God to drive away evil and obtain what is good. Contemplation is when the mind is in some sort lifted up to God and held above itself, so that it tastes the joys of everlasting sweetness.

So the soul, seeing that it cannot attain by itself that sweetness of knowing and feeling for which it longs, and that the more the heart abases itself, the more God is exalted, humbles itself and betakes itself to prayer, saying: Lord, you are not seen except by the pure of heart. I seek by reading and meditating what is true purity of heart and how it may be attained, so that with its help I may know you, if only a little. Lord, for long have I meditated in my heart, seeking to see your face. It is the sight of you, Lord, that I have sought; and all the while in my meditation the fire of longing, the desire to know you more fully, has increased. When you break the bread of sacred Scripture for me, you have shown yourself to me in that breaking of bread, and the more I see you, the more I long to see you. Nor do I ask this, Lord, because of my own merits, but because of your mercy. I too in my unworthiness confess my sins like the woman who said that 'even the little dogs eat of the fragments that fall from the table of their masters.' So give me, Lord, some pledge of what I hope to inherit, at least one drop of heavenly rain with which to refresh my thirst, for I am on fire with love.

So the soul by such burning words inflames its own desire, makes known its state, and by such spells it seeks to call its spouse. But the Lord, whose eyes are upon the just and whose ears can catch not only the words but the very meaning of their prayers, does not wait until the longing soul has said all its say, but breaks in upon the middle of its prayer, runs to meet it with all haste, sprinkled with sweet heavenly dew, anointed with the most precious perfumes, and he restores the weary soul, he slakes its thirst, he feeds its hunger, he makes the soul forget all earthly things: by making it die to itself he gives it new life in a wonderful way, and by making it drunk he brings it back to its true senses.

Let him sit alone, the Scripture says; and indeed, unless he sits and rests, he will not be alone. So it is good to be humbled, Lord, and to bear your burden. By carrying your burden the proud learn meekness. And you say to those who take up your burden: 'Learn from me, for I am meek and humble of heart.' He who is filled with pride does not know how to sit still. But your throne is humility and peace. And now I see that no one can be at peace until he has become humble. Humility and peace: how good it is for a man to be humbled so that he can attain to peace. Then indeed will he sit alone and be silent. He who is not alone cannot be silent. And he who is not silent cannot hear you when you speak to him.

Then when man realizes that he may not reach the knowledge or the feeling of wisdom through himself, the more he will strive to attain it. The more he sees what the Godhead does; then does he see that his might and his wit are as nothing and begins to know himself, and as a poor wretch humbles himself and drops down with a meek heart to pray and say: Lord, you that will not be seen except by those that are clean of heart, I have done what I can, read and deeply thought and searched for the way I might best come to this cleanness that I might some day know you. Lord, I have sought and thought with all my poor heart; and, Lord, in my meditation lies the fire of desire to know you not superficially but in the very depth of my soul. Lord, this worthiness I ask not as I am, for I am wretched and sinful and most unworthy, but as much, Lord, as a dog eats the crumbs that fall from the table of the lord, I ask of the heritage that is to come one drop of that heavenly joy to comfort my thirsty soul that burneth in lovelonging for you.

Guiges du Pont

If you desire to know what God is, since you cannot love what you know nothing of, consider spiritually, in simplicity of heart, as far as possible, with the help of grace, that God is the first and supreme essence, the supreme and perfect nature, the supreme majesty, the supreme power, the supreme goodness, the supreme knowledge, the supreme wisdom, the supreme truth, the supreme mercy, the supreme justice, the supreme kindness, the supreme compassion, the supreme light, the supreme splendour, the supreme beatitude, the supreme peace, the supreme virtue, the supreme eternity, the supreme charity, the source of all life, the supreme and greatest creator, preserver and lover of all the visible and invisible things which are good, the principle of all existing things.

In order that the image of God, which is the soul of man, may be pure so as to attend to God and to remain united to its Creator, it is necessary that the contemplative should abstain from material affairs as far as is possible. Hence, whoever thirsts to contemplate God should avoid worldly things: for if he does not, he will be full of the caprices of the world and cannot possibly have a serene heart, tranquil and prepared to receive, with pure and spiritual taste.

Since the exercise of contemplation, properly of the angels, is above human science and virtue, no one can arrive at it without the help and preparation of divine grace. It seems clear that unceasing prayer is very necessary in order to obtain continual grace. In time this prayer becomes a humble and familiar conversation with God, who does not turn us away as being unworthy, but desires to be with us. Prayer is a good contemplation, which brings us nearer and advances us in the knowledge and love of God.

Hugh of Balma

Threefold is the way which leads to God. The first is the purgative way, in which the mind is disposed to learn true wisdom. The second is called the illuminative way, in which the mind by meditating enkindles in itself the flame of love. The third is the unitive way, in which the mind, beyond all knowledge, consideration and understanding, is raised up on high directly by God alone.

The soul commences with an imperfect love. By the exercise of meditation it arrives at the perfection of love. Then, strengthened by continual exercise in the unitive way, it is lifted up above itself by the right hand of its Creator. Owing to its frequent acts of love and pious ejaculations it is overtaken with the keenest desire to possess God, and much sooner than might be imagined, without any previous or accompanying reflection.

Mystical wisdom derives from an ardent desire to abandon normal intellectual functions so that divine insight may enlighten this ardour and add to it another fire, much stronger, which lifts the burning soul towards an even deeper wisdom.

3

Fourteenth Century

Ludolph of Saxony
(b. circa 1259; d. 1378)
Member of the Community of the Strasbourg Charterhouse

Henry Egher of Kalkar
(b. 1328; d. 1408)
Prior of Cologne and Strasbourg Charterhouses

Nicholas Kempf
(b. 1393 in Strasbourg)
Member of Gairach, Garning and Pleterje Charterhouse
communities (1437–68)

Margaret D'Oyngt
Prioress of Poleteins Charterhouse, France (1288–1310)

Anonymous
(Carthusian of Treves)

Ludolph of Saxony

O most sweet Lord Jesus Christ, pour forth, I beseech you, the abundance of your love on me a sinner, so that I may desire nothing earthly, nothing carnal, but may love you alone above all things, and that my soul may entirely refuse to be comforted except by you, my sweet Lord and God. Write with your finger on the tablets of my heart the remembrance of what you have endured for me, that I may have this always before my eyes, and it may be sweet for me not merely to think about it but also to bear what you endured in my own way. May I only serve you with all my strength.

O Jesus, when dying for us on the Cross, you willed that your side should be opened by a spear, so that blood and water, emblems of the Sacraments, might flow out. I beseech you to wound my heart with the spear of divine love, that I may be worthy to receive the Sacraments which flow from your most holy side. Everyone desiring to pray devoutly ought to have three attributes, namely, a firm faith, signified by Peter; abandonment of worldly goods, trampling them contemptuously underfoot and not thinking of them at all whilst praying, typified by James, who is called the supplanter; and the fervent state of grace in which we must be and which is shown by John, representing 'he in whom grace dwells'.

Meditating on the psalms has this advantage: it brings to the forefront of the mind all that is contained in the Old and New Testaments. When singing or reciting the psalms devoutly one has the joy of Jesus being present. They generate a glowing affection and purify with the sword of the Spirit which is the Word of God . . . In the psalms you will find help in adversity and be able to express thanksgiving. Whoever succeeds by the grace of God to absorb them thoroughly perceives every divine virtue in them. St Augustine speaks of the excellence of the psalms and of their ability to enlighten the mind. They bring tranquillity to the soul and are bearers of peace.

Even the most ignorant can become wise through frequent meditation of the Passion but wisdom alone is not enough: it is charity which edifies. Meditation is a way of life in which all that is necessary for salvation can be found. Happy is the one who studies seriously because he will increase his desire to distance himself from the world and involve himself in the love of God while at the same time acquiring heavenly virtues. Meditation on the Passion should not be made superficially nor in haste but on suitable occasion when one has sufficient time.

Just as vanity is detested both by God and man, so is humility pleasing to God and man. He who is humble is full of charity, affable and helpful. In order to be humble in this way, let us diligently consider the humility of Jesus Christ who, although being King of kings, true God and the only begotten Son of the Father, lived in this world in true humility so that we might imitate him.

Henry Egher of Kalkar

I beseech you to receive me and to preserve me from all sin. May my soul be united to you, O my God, by the most perfect, most fervent, most faithful and unceasing love, so that with all my heart and from the depths of my soul, I may love you, seek you, long for you, praise and bless you in all things and above all things. May I spend my whole life and all the powers of my body and soul in praising, honouring and serving you.

Nicholas Kempf

O my beloved Jesus, you have opened your heart to
me that I may enter there at will. And so that I may
be able more surely to come to you through your Passion
and your wounds, you stretch out your arms and hasten
to meet me, always ready to receive me just as the hen
gathers her little ones under her wings.

Margaret D'Oyngt

Lord sweet Jesus, I shall never be in peace until I know how to love you with all my heart. There is nothing in the world which I desire more than this. Sweet Lord, for love of you I have left father, mother, brothers and all in this world. Yet, this is as nothing since the riches of this world are nothing more than prickly thorns: the more one has the more unfortunate one is! You know, Lord, that if I possessed a thousand worlds and could dispose of them as I liked, I would leave all for your love. Moreover, even if you gave me all that you possess in heaven and earth, I would not feel satisfied without you. You are my life and I wish for no father or mother apart from you.

Certainly if one considers the beauty and the goodness which are in God, one would love him so much that everything else would seem wretched: he is willing to share this sweetness and kindness with us . . . God is so great that he is everywhere and those who love him can be with him wherever they are. In effect, the Lord is with them wherever they are . . . God is omnipotent and for this reason he has given of his power and energy to those who love him.

God is imperturbable and there cannot be any weakness in him. He is supreme joy and there is no joy or loving kindness which does not come from him. He is so good that those who have tasted that goodness hunger so much for his goodness that they never think of wanting anything more than the love to be found in his goodness. God is all-wise and has given such wisdom to

Fourteenth Century

33

those that love him that they never need to ask for it. God is love and is eternal and because of that he has enfolded to himself those who love him so that they will live eternally with him.

The times are so uncertain; although I am here today I know not where I shall be tomorrow and no one is sure of his salvation. I only know, O sweet Jesus, that your words are true. Since you assure me that you love those who love you, I do all I can to love you.

O sweet Lord, it seems to me that nature demands man to love his parents, brothers, sisters, friends, his spouse and those who are kind to him. Yet, dear Lord, if I love my father who is but a mortal, how much more should I love you who are my spiritual father and my eternal life. O Lord God, be not offended if I call you father, since you created me, giving me a soul and body and out of your mercy making me in your image and likeness.

O Lord God, now I see that there is nothing so precious and of such worth as the soul of a man or a woman. You are the true Wisdom in whom is all knowledge and of whose riches the heavenly paradise is full. It was not enough for you to descend from heaven to earth where you suffered so many pains and suffered so many indignities; you decided to shed your blood for us on account of your great love for us.

When I consider your kindnesses, which are so many, so great and so full of love, I think that if the worst man in the world reflected and meditated on them, he would be converted to faith in you immediately. Sweet Lord, I don't know what else to do except to think over and over again of all the graces and favours you have conferred on me. Grant me, gracious Jesus, the grace to understand and meditate on them so that I may acquire your holy love.

Anonymous (A Carthusian of Treves)

Truly, all the blessings we can desire come most abundantly from Jesus, and every grace we receive is poured out upon us from no other source than that of his Heart, sweeter than honey. His Heart is the furnace of divine love, always burning with the fire of the Holy Spirit and purifying, kindling and transforming into himself all who yield themselves to him, or who wish to be his.

Since all good flows from the most sweet Heart of Jesus, you must offer back to his Heart all the gifts, graces and blessings which have been bestowed upon you and upon all men. You should do this for the greater glory of God and for the benefit of the Holy Church, not attributing to yourself anything of the good you may have done, not regarding with self-satisfaction the gifts of God, but ascribing all to him and returning all to their original source, which is the Heart of Jesus. Make this offering especially when you say the Gloria Patri or recite psalms and hymns which speak of the glory of God.

4

Fifteenth Century

Denys the Carthusian
(b. circa 1402; d. 1471)
Member of the Community of the Roermand Charterhouse in
Holland

Dominic of Treves
(b. 1328; d. 1408)
Member of the Communities of the Sierk and Treves
Charterhouses in Germany

Anonymous Carthusian
Member of the Community of Nuremberg Charterhouse
(circa 1480)

Henry Arnoldi
(d. 1487)
Prior of Basle Charterhouse

James of Clusa
(d. 1466)
Member of the Community of the Erfurt Charterhouse,
Germany; former Abbot in the Cistercian Order

Nicholas Love
Prior of Mount Grace Charterhouse, England (1410–21)

Denys the Carthusian

You must think of the joys of the heavenly kingdom, and speak thus within your soul:

My soul, how great and what priceless happiness and glory will it be to see the God of infinite beauty face to face, and to abide with him in the depths of his sweetness. Think what it will be like to belong for ever with the almighty changeless God! In him, happily to hold and to possess, in overflowing measure, the fullness of all beauty, and of all that can be wished: yes, and safe in eternity to have your heart's wish; ah! think what it will be! To taste the peace of God which he has created, to plumb the depths of the sweetness of his love! What will it be like, O my soul, to be wrapped up in the love of the Creator, to be made a partaker in the Godhead – how thrilling and how much to be sought after! And then, to be closely locked in God's most loving arms, so that no one can ever tear you away from the glowing gaze of his joyous countenance, nor from the embrace of his love!

'Dearest brothers, let us simplify our hearts, discounting all affections for carnal and transient things, and concentrate on that divine good which never changes. For this one thing alone is needed – to attain perfection through Godlike simplification: a continuing and loving conversion of the spirit towards divine simplicity, in which we are all most closely and purely united, so that we are further from and as much separated as is possible from all that is of this world and can attend to divine things alone, pure and fervent . . .

What can be more wonderful in this life than to be

free for God above all other things, and to cling to him with a tranquil and sincere soul; to be rid of the tumults of the world, from the worries of this life and the bitter passions of anger, impatience, fear, self-pity – and then begin to pursue in cell a heavenly life, thus enjoying even in this life a foretaste of the delights of future bliss?'

O Lord Jesus Christ, in union with the praises you have offered to God for all eternity, I now desire to offer up these praises and prayers, beseeching you through your infinite mercy to give me a contrite and devout heart, a very humble and pure heart, a very fervent and faithful heart, a heart like yours; a heart that you will keep holy, that you will bind to yourself – your heart. May I be attached to you alone, see and seek only you; may ever bless, praise and love you in all things. Sweet Jesus, grant me the grace to pray with that attention and devotion which will enable me to fulfil your wishes and the commands of the Church, and that through your mercy for the living and the dead, redeemed by your blood, I may obtain the fruits of your Passion and death.

Only Son of the Eternal Father, O you in whom the Father is well pleased, it is you who fulfilled the wonderful and merciful decrees of the Blessed Trinity, and who in accordance with your ardent charity and your ineffable goodness, vouchsafed to descend from the bosom, or rather, the heart of your Father, to become incarnate in the womb of a most pure virgin, in order to render honour and obedience to God, and to procure the salvation of mankind. O Christ, mighty Lord, most sweet

Jesus, my strength and my refuge, defender of my soul, God of my salvation, it is you in whom I believe and hope, you whom I love. I draw near to your throne of grace, I knock at the door of your mercy, and beseech you to open it to me. You who promised entrance into Paradise to the penitent thief, bring me through the most holy wound of your side to the centre of your heart, and let me drink at the fountain of wisdom that flows from it. O God of infinite mercy, receive me, enclose me and hide me in the bosom of your mercy.

After God, it is to Mary that we owe our existence. We were created because of her, and because of her divine Son. As a result of man's first sin, the divine Justice claimed its rights; and if the divine Mercy triumphed over its demands, it is thanks to Mary. She intervened in our favour, and begged the sovereign Judge to give us time in which to repent and do penance.

Love and gratitude are due to the privileged one who has obtained so much for us. Bless her, as the ship-wrecked mariner blesses the charitable hand which draws him to the shore; as the prisoner blesses his liberator, and the condemned man his saviour.

You are the consolation and the hope of the most guilty of men. He who has recourse to you can never complain of your severity and harshness. To your sons, even to the most ungrateful, you are kindness and tenderness itself; for all you have the heart of a compassionate and indulgent Mother. Despite the high estate you enjoy in heaven, if the most wretched, the most impure, the most despised of sinners appeals to you for help with a truly contrite and humbled heart, far from disdaining him you welcome him with a mother's love. You take him into your arms and, holding him close to your heart, you communicate to him a new warmth and then make his peace with the Judge he fears. How many are the afflicted, the sinners, the utterly abandoned, who rejoice that they have found in you, O Mary most merciful, salvation and life!

Dominic of Treves

Offer what you have received to the Heart of Jesus through the blessed hands of his Mother. Pray to her that her maternal goodness may help you, so that, with all the saints and elect of God, you may praise and bless the Lord for all the benefits he has bestowed upon you down to the present time and for all those he will grant for all eternity.

Anonymous (A Carthusian of Nuremberg)

The Heart of Jesus is the source of the divine river springing up in the midst of Paradise to water the surface of the earth, to quench the thirst of the dry and barren human heart, to wash away sin, to extinguish the unholy fires of greed, to control the flights of the imagination and to allay the fierceness of anger. Draw near then and take the draught of love from this fountain of the Saviour, in order that you may no longer live for yourself but in him.

O all-glorious and most amiable Jesus, Creator of the mysterious and invisible world of grace, guest of loving hearts, crucified example of souls crushed under the weight of the cross, in you are contained all the riches and all the gifts of heaven. Jesus our King, Saviour of the faithful, who willed that your holy side should be opened by the point of a ruthless lance, I humbly and fervently beseech you to open the doors of your mercy to me and allow me to enter through the large wound of your most holy side, into your infinitely loving Heart, so that my heart may be united to your Heart by an indissoluble bond of love. Wound my heart with your love; let the soldier's spear penetrate my breast. May my heart be opened to you alone and closed to the world and the devil. Protect my heart, and arm it against the assaults of its enemies by the sign of your holy cross.

Henry Arnoldi

Behold and see, says Our Lord Jesus Christ, what a painful position I am in upon the cross. My arms are extended in order to be always able to receive and embrace you each time you come to me. My feet are nailed, that you may know that I cannot, will not, be parted from you. My hands, since they are pierced through and through, show you that it would be impossible for them, even when closed, to withhold the favours you seek from me. But understand that it is not the nails that fasten me to the cross and keep me there but my love. I have loved you throughout all eternity, and will love you eternally, so long as you never cease to love me. I will never forget you. Deeply, carefully, and lovingly have I wrapped you in the wounds of my feet and hands. I have even gone further; as if this were not enough I have had my side pierced by a soldier's spear in order to open wide for you the entrance to my heart, and to show you how great was the love which led me to die for you.

Desiring more easily to attract and keep you close to me by the bonds of love, I have caused blood and water to flow from my side after death. Blood to pay your ransom, water to wash away your sins. In this way, by virtue of the Sacraments contained in this blood and this water, I have set you free and renewed your innocence.

James of Clusa

Should courage fail us when we have some work to do, let us look at the wounded hands of Jesus. Should we feel weak when we have afflictions to bear, let us contemplate the feet of Jesus, pierced with nails and bathed in blood. Yes, let us look at those feet which support the weight of the whole body.

Nicholas Love

I beseech you, sweet Jesus, in all your goodness, graciously to visit my sick soul this day, as I long to receive you and all your graces, that I may happily find body and soul healed by your presence. Look not, Lord Jesus, on my wickedness, nor on my neglect of you and my great unkindness, but rather send down your mercy and endless goodness. Truly you are the sinless holy lamb offered to the everlasting Father in heaven for the redemption of the world ... And at the last, grant that with a blessed departing from this wretched world I may come to life everlasting with you, Lord Jesus, by virtue and grace of your blessed life without ending.

5

Sixteenth Century

Michael of Coutances
Forty-ninth Prior of the Grande Chartreuse (1594–1600)

John of Torralba
(d. 1578)
Prior of Aula Dei Charterhouse, Spain

Anthony Volmar
(b. circa 1550)
Prior of Astheim Charterhouse, Germany

John Lanspergus
(b. 1490; d. 1539)
Prior of Julich Charterhouse, Germany (1530–5)

Michael of Coutances

A faithful soul should imitate a beggar. It should cast itself in spirit before God, as another Lazarus, covered with sores, yet filled with desire to be satisfied with the crumbs from the bread which fall from his table. Let it uncover before him its miseries and its needs, knowing well by faith that God understands better than itself what is most fitting for it, and being convinced by hope that he has the will to give the same. If words fail, the soul has only to persevere in remaining before God with patience and humility, and to be content to re-expose its needs from time to time with confidence. It was in this way that our beloved Lord and Master Jesus Christ acted during his prayer in the Garden.

I say that the prayer of abandonment to the good pleasure of God is the best of all, and the most sure. Now I call prayer of abandonment:

1. that which is made without philosophizing too much about its name and about its qualities, since it is sufficient to know that all comes from God, and that all should be attributed to him;

2. which only tends to abase oneself before God in order to unite oneself to him;

3. which is in indifference about being placed high or low, according to the place and position he will desire to give;

4. and which desires nothing save the consummation of his holy love. That contains virtually all the others, and all the others only increase in perfection in proportion as it is found in them.

Grant then that we may make all our prayers:

1. *Lovingly*, for your sake and your love, that, as you desire, we may please you in this, and offer you acceptable service. May your will, should we ask and obtain something from you, move us to pray more that our desire for progress in our love for you be furthered by our prayers.

2. May we pray *purely*, without attraction towards any sin, avoiding our affection from every sin.

3. May we pray *faithfully*, believing that you have the power and the will to hear us favourably.

4. May we pray *humbly*, recognizing that we deserve not to be heard, on account of our ingratitude, infidelity, neglect and manifold sins.

5. May we pray *beseechingly*, supplicating to be heard, for your goodness and other perfections, the merit of your life and Passion, and the intercessions of the Saints.

6. May we pray *confidently*, with the hope of being heard this way.

7. May we pray *efficaciously*, making use of the means which lie within us, of our own efforts together with your grace, and applying and using human remedies.

8. May we pray *fervently* and with *integrity*, not with a divided, tepid and distracted heart, but recollected with all our might, and attentive and fervent in our prayer.

9. May we pray with *forbearance* and *courage*, persevering in prayer even in the time of aridity and not abandoning the desire and hope of being answered, however long you may defer the granting of that which you know is for our good.

10. May we pray with *resignation*, fully committed to the reply of your paternal will and perfectly conforming

ourselves to it, whether you hear us soon or late, and even if you refuse to grant that for which we pray.

Remember, O most merciful Jesus, all the favours and mercies you have shown towards us; remember your pains, the wounds you have received, all the blood you have shed; and finally the very bitter death you accepted for us. In consideration of all that I have reminded you, I beseech you to pour out on the souls in Purgatory the virtue, efficacy, fruit and merit of your sufferings and your Passion, in order that each soul there may be entirely released, or at least greatly relieved. O Jesus, remember that these souls are your friends, your children, your chosen, whom you have redeemed. Let your justice be satisfied with the grievous punishment they have endured until now. For your own sake, O Lord, show mercy and remit the rest of their sufferings.

And then, O sweet Jesus, if it can contribute to your glory, grant that I may pass from this life straight into life eternal. But O my God, if you have otherwise decreed, and the contrary is for your greater glory, I resign and give myself into your loving hands. Do with me as you wish, most loving, most faithful and most merciful Lord Jesus.

O you who art the one true and most faithful friend of my soul, Lord Jesus Christ, Son of God and of the most compassionate Virgin Mary; O God supremely worthy of infinite love and adoration, in union with the love of your most loving Mother, and of the angels and saints in Paradise, in my own name and in that of your friends and mine, in the name of the whole Church, militant and suffering, I offer you your own most gentle Heart, and through it I adore you in union with the Father and the Holy Ghost. It is through your Heart that I praise and glorify you, that I love you and give thanks to you.

O good Jesus, never did you pass over so painful a road as that which led to Calvary; never have you borne on your shoulders a load to be compared with that of the Cross. By all the anguish of your Heart and all the sufferings of your body, I beseech you that in carrying my cross I may neither waver nor fall, but may advance towards perfection, always tending towards a better end. May I deal with all things with discretion, and may I be submissive to my superiors in humility of heart, trusting more in others than in myself. I do not mean, like Simon the Cyrenian, to follow you by compulsion, but to follow you willingly, with loving imitation, and to remain ever united to you in endless charity.

O Lord Jesus, I offer you the prayers of this day, also my thoughts, desires, words and actions, my sufferings and my merits. I offer all to you only for love of you and that I may please you by doing your will. I desire to act under your infinitely wise direction and according to your intentions, through you and with you. With the help of your most gentle Heart, I will begin, continue and end my prayers, and offer them to you in union with the very perfect praises and the infinite love with which the three Persons of the most holy Trinity mutually praise and love each other.

I unite myself also to the infinite charity which, from

the most holy Trinity, descends into your human heart, O Word made Man, and which re-ascends from your heart to the bosom of the same most perfect Trinity.

O most sweet Jesus, by the sweetness of your Heart, I beseech you to fill me and all other souls with a very great fervent and a very perfect unceasing love. That love will make us ardently seek your glory. We shall then grow holier and remain steadfast in friendship with you.

John of Torralba

You have subjected the natural love for your humanity to the love of the divinity and have been obedient to your Father, even to dying on the Cross. Give to me the same grace, in order that I may renounce my own will, think not of myself, and be in perfect submission to God and to all creatures for his sake.

Make my heart so true, so upright, so pure, so in unison with your Heart, that there may be nothing to offend you or estrange you from me. In all my words and actions, may I seek and have only one thing in view: namely, to please and honour you. I desire to do all that is pleasing to you. I wish to love you with all my heart; my unceasing care will be to repay to you at least some of the love so evident in your great charity.

O Jesus, who is loving kindness itself, from this throne of grace and pardon, the Cross, to which I behold you fastened, send me your Spirit. He will teach me to give proof of my gratitude, to make my life more like yours, to take part in your sufferings and death. He will show me how to return to you love for love, and how to remain ever faithful to you, who has redeemed me at such great cost.

Anthony Volmar

The bee that flies further than the others and hovers over more flowers, collects their juices in greater abundance and makes more honey. Thus is the soul that is frequently lifted up by mental prayer to this most beautiful flower of the field, Jesus, loaded with shame and covered with wounds. The soul that extends the breadth of its contemplation and considers more attentively the sufferings of Jesus, better understands each of the Saviour's wounds and finds honey in the openings of the mystical rock, which is Christ himself. I will turn then to Jesus all covered with wounds. I will never cease my endeavours to reach him until my soul shall be united with his soul, my spirit to his spirit, and my heart to his Heart. Jesus is himself the light and the way that leads to himself. Jesus, as a light in a lantern, will be my guide. The light of his divinity is set in his humanity and streams out from his many wounds.

John Lanspergus

You should be so poor in spirit that there should be nothing you did love or dislike, reject or plead for, fear or desire personally in any respect. Instead only fulfil my will which at all times and in all places you will, in wonder, come to understand from those things which I ordain and permit, if you seek me with a pure mind and have faith in me.

You have understood sufficiently how you ought to be patient and meek; how you should bear all things with an indifferent, peaceable and quiet mind (for meekness is nothing other than perfect tranquillity in true patience) so that nothing should be able to make you sad, or worry or trouble you, whatever happens to you unless it be a result of God's displeasure.

What shall I render unto you, O gracious Lover, for that most bitter death which you suffered for me and for that unspeakable charity which you showed towards me? O good Jesus, enable me, I beseech you, to share all your worthiness.

O most gracious and loving Lord, enliven me and revive me with God's grace, separate me wholly from all evil, and convert me altogether to you. Grant that I may hate that which you hate and love that which you love. Never cease to help me to increase abundantly in all virtues.

In making Mary the treasurer of his grace, Christ our Lord has willed that we should receive through her all that we ask of him, although he can give it to us directly himself. It is in this way that the poor and afflicted of this world receive from the hands of the royal treasurer the alms that the King is desirous of giving to them.

'In the Carthusian Order, you have both the eremitical and cenobitic lives, and both of them so tempered by the Holy Ghost, that whatever in both of them might be dangerous is removed and whatever conduces to progress and perfection in both lives, is preserved for you. Solitude such as you will find in the Charterhouse, is free from any indiscretion or danger. First of all, because those who have made profession of it must live not according to their own whims, but under obedience and the rule of their Superiors. Again, they are not so much left to their own devices that they cannot have help, attendance and service when they have need of them. And yet, their solitude is truly anchoritical on account of the perfect observance of silence, so that if you will, you may dwell there hidden in the deepest depths of solitude. For what matters it whether you have many or few companions in your solitude? What does it matter whether you live in solitude alone or have many at your side? What does solitude lose or gain whether you dwell alone in a forest or in the cloister, provided you persevere in silence? So that this Carthusian solitude to which you are called, is not less real than that of the primitive anchorites, provided as I have said, that like them you work alone.'

Sixteenth Century

59

6

Seventeenth Century

Innocent Le Masson
(b. 1628; d. 1703)
Prior of the Grande Chartreuse (1675–1703)

John Anadaon
(d. 1682)
Prior of Aula Dei, Spain

Polycarp de la Riviere
(b. circa 1550)
Prior of Bordeaux (1628) and Bompas Charterhouses in France

Anthony de Molina
(d. 1612)
Member of the Community of Miraflores Charterhouse, Spain

Renatus Hansaeus
Prior of Brno Charterhouse, Moravia in 1610, former Member
of the Grande Chartreuse

Laurence Wartenberger
(b. circa 1590)
Prior of the Coblenz Charterhouse

The pursuit of love and virtue begins to make us virtuous, but the pursuit and love of honour begins to make us abject and contemptible. Generous spirits busy not themselves about these poor toys.

Many will not dare think about the graces God has given them in particular, fearing that thereby they may fall into vainglory and self-conceit; but, in truth, they deceive themselves. The true means to attain to the love of God, as says the great Angelical Doctor, is the consideration of his benefits; the more we know them, the more we shall love him . . . Certainly nothing can so much humble us before the mercy of God as the multitude of his gifts, nor before his justice as the multitude of our offences. Let us then consider what he has done for us and what we have done against him. As we consider our sins one by one, so let us consider his graces one by one.

Let us consider those small temptations of vanity, suspicion, anxiety, jealousy, envy, coquetry and such trifles which like flies or gnats, hover before our eyes and sometimes sting us upon the cheek and sometimes upon the nose. It is impossible to be altogether free from their importunity; the best resistance we can offer is not to worry about them. Although they may trouble us, they cannot hurt us if we are thoroughly determined to serve God.

For the love of God contains in itself the perfection of

all virtues, and far greater than the virtues themselves, is also a more sovereign remedy against all vices.

We should enter into conversation with God without troubling about the composition of our words . . . Those souls which are completely occupied by God have nothing to say since their interior being is everything and contains everything they could wish to say.

The heart is good that has good affections, and the affections and passions are good which bring forth in us good effects and holy actions. If this softness, this tenderness, and these consolations make us more humble, patient, tractable, charitable, and compassionate towards our neighbour, more fervent in mortifying our concupiscence and sinful inclinations, more constant in our exercises, more meek and pliable to those whom we ought to obey, more sincere in our lives, then without doubt they are from God.

Let us receive graces and favours, humbly valuing them as exceedingly precious, not so much because they are so in themselves, as because it is the hand of God which infuses them into our hearts, as a loving mother would do who, with love for her child, puts sugar-plums into his mouth with her own hand, one by one; if the child has wisdom, he would care more for the sweetness of his mother's fondling and caresses than for the sweetness of the sugar-plums themselves.

Remember that you need his help just as much as if you had never before experienced it: you owe his love as much respect and gratitude as if you had never yet paid any at all; you are as much bound to do your best to please him as if you had never done anything before for him. In your heavenly Father's bosom repeat David's words: 'And now I resolve to begin afresh', applying them to the renewed grace that you expect from him, to the fresh assistance you are going to receive, and to the resolution you have made of beginning afresh with renewed zeal in his love, as though you had never yet done anything for him.

Lying in his bosom, think of yourself as mere nothingness, which you would always remain unless your heavenly Father's love uplifted you afresh. Lay before him your wishes and requests with a confidence as great as his love, and be sure that, with the gift of a new being, his love assures you also that it will act as though only beginning: it is about to be showered upon you afresh, as though it had never done anything for you, in the same way as it makes the sun shine upon you as though it had never happened before.

Then think of yourself as something newly brought out of nothingness, and placed under the unfailing protection of its All. Say to yourself that, leaving your heavenly Father's bosom, you take up two wings, confidence and humility, which must serve constantly to keep you balanced between heaven and earth.

Solitude of soul implies the cutting off of every attachment, so that the soul remains voluntarily stripped, not only of its affection, desires and cares, but even of itself. It no longer considers its own consolation, its own profit or happiness, but God alone! It is his glory that is its aim; all else is naught.

The bee, says Aristotle, takes honey from the flowers without hurting them, leaving them as entire and fresh as it found them; but true devotion goes yet further, for it not only does not prejudice any sort of vocation or employment, but, on the contrary, adorns and beautifies it. Wheresoever we are, we may and ought to aspire to a perfect life. Each one should conduct himself in his own state of life, and become all things to all men according to the right order of charity.

What gain there will be for those who leave all things for God, as religious should. In order to work out our salvation securely, we should quit the wide road of the world whereon many walk, whose wills are said to be good yet produce no results. We should often turn to the example of the saints, for they kindle the desire to practise virtue. A soul wishing to adhere wholly to God, ought to be intent on all that leads to great sanctity and perfection. Seclusion and solitude are most conducive to pleasing God, and the avoidance of the dangers and troubles of life.

When you rise from your meditation, remember the resolutions and deliberations you have taken, and carefully put them into practice that day. This is the chief fruit of meditation, without which it is often not only unprofitable but hurtful, for virtues meditated and not practised puff up the mind, and make us think that we are such indeed as we are resolved to be. Doubtless this is true, when our resolutions are lively and solid; yet rather in vain and dangerous, if they are not put into practice. We must therefore try all means and seek all occasions, little or great, to put our resolutions into effect. For example, if I resolved by mildness to win the minds of those who may have offended me, I must endeavour to meet them without delay and greet them courteously, or if I cannot meet with them, to speak well of them and to pray to God for them.

When you have finished mental prayer take care not to give your heart a jog, lest you spill the balm you have received through your prayer. By this I mean, if it is possible, remain silent for some time and gently and slowly turn your heart from your prayers to your worldly business, retaining so long as you are able the feeling and affection you attained.

Many imagine that there are great mysteries in the exercise of mental prayer. Some believe that it is only possible for those who have retired into solitude: others, thinking it is an art which can be made use of at pleasure once its secret has been discovered, encumber their mind with a quantity of reading and ideas. However, they deceive themselves: for there is nothing so easy as prayer, nothing so possible for all kinds of people, whoever they may be; nothing so far removed from all artifice.

The grace of meditation, as St Francis of Sales says, cannot be acquired by any human labour. When it so pleases God, he gives it; yet only to souls who are humble, and who continue to present themselves before him with the intention of saying to him the best they can, abandoning themselves for the rest to the dispositions of his providence. By this grace of meditation is to be understood the facility of raising and uniting the soul to God.

In order to draw profit from prayer, one needs calm gentleness and suavity of spirit, and these spring from the knowledge of our own insufficiency and true humility. For if we acknowledge the truth and are convinced that we are unable to pray as we ought, unless the Holy Ghost teaches us, we shall clearly see that over-eagerness is altogether useless. All that we have to do is to place ourselves in the presence of God with confidence, without eagerness for success, and remain there in all humility, expressing to his divine Majesty our affections and needs in tranquillity the best we may.

By faith the soul should be persuaded that God is every-where, and knows all things, and therefore knows all its necessities before it asks. But divine providence, which could very well provide for all its needs without the soul being under the necessity of asking for them, has ordained that it should lay them open in prayer, so that there may be petition; and also that the soul may render that submission which is due to God.

Where, O my soul, are you about to place yourself? – Before God, whom I believe to be more present here than myself; who knows all my needs, but who wills that I should ask them from him.

What do you hope for from him? – All the necessary help to please him, and to come to him.

Again, what do you desire? – Nothing more than his love, his fear and the happiness of being eternally united to him.

If we feel that our conscience answers to us in this

way on these questions, our soul is in the posture it should be in before God.

But note that there is no need to form an idea of something physical representing God in the imagination: on the contrary, if one forms by itself, it must be rejected as it has no relationship to God, who is pure spirit. Nevertheless, that should be done gently, little by little, so as not to fall into over-eagerness. Doubtless a spirit which is still only accustomed to work on material objects, becomes astonished when its ideas are taken away from it all at once. But once it has gently become used to this, it will realize that there is nothing more in conformity with its nature, and it will receive great joy therefrom.

Speak to God freely, for he hears you. Do not go to seek him anywhere else than in the centre of your heart, since he is assuredly there. To see God in oneself, and to accustom oneself to regard him by faith, and not by fancy; to speak to him with confidence, as being in the centre of your heart, without going to the trouble of seeking him elsewhere; such is the way to learn quickly to walk in spirit, to reach to the truth and to attain easy familiarity with the person of God.

We should enter into conversation with God without troubling about the composition of our words, nor making much account of the continuity of the conversation. To do so would be harmful for the affections, and it tends rather to study than to the production of that sincerity of a heart which comes to pour itself out before God.

Let us be content to have recourse in good faith to moderate resolutions, in particular to correct some fault which we remark in ourselves, or to practise some act of virtue the best we can. Let us not become over-anxious but watch ourselves with the gentleness of confidence in God, so as not to fall into such excesses of anxiety which are detrimental to nature and to the progress of virtue. One does not climb to the top of the mountain all at once; one must go there step by step. The perfect practice of a virtue is not the work of a day; we have to climb the steps, we slip and have to pick ourselves up again before reaching the top.

John Anadaon

Contemplate this wound of the Sacred Heart, for therein is the source of our life. There indeed has our heavenly Father regenerated us for the life of heaven. There we see unfolded for our contemplation the incomprehensible love of Jesus for us, for we see him wholly immolated for us. He has reserved nothing for himself but has offered all for us. What more could he do? He has opened to us the hidden sanctuary of his Heart and he introduces us as his intimate friends. For his delight is to be with us in silent peace and peaceful silence.

Polycarp de la Riviere

For what are you doing, my soul, in offering your heart for that of your God? Would you live without a heart, and shut yourself out of heaven? To enjoy the latter, it is necessary to open the former. I know you will say that it is from this divine Heart, and not from heaven, that you have taken your very essence, and that you cannot do without its love, for you are like the moon, which of itself is not visible and sends forth no light which it does not receive from the sun. But reflect also that the Heart of Jesus performs all things with harmony and consideration, and that, being the first of the living and the dead, the chief of the elect, and the prototype of all perfection, it must needs be opened in order to become the door to Paradise.

Let the good things of this world vanish away. They are only mire, scum and corruption, perpetual figures of death, and not to be compared to the greatness of my love which only longs for and clings to this Heart of my soul, to this soul of my heart.

Anthony De Molina

Notice that the Evangelist does not say that the soldier struck, tore or wounded the side of Jesus, but that he opened it. He uses this expression to make us understand why Our Lord chose to receive this thrust. By opening to us his Heart, Jesus wished to reveal to us the very great love with which he burns for us, and to show us that all he has suffered he has suffered because his Heart was wounded with love of souls; and to prove this he had his Heart opened and left ever open, so that, through this wide door, we may reach the centre of his Heart, and find a place of refuge from temptations and dangers.

Renatus Hansaeus

Enter then through this gate of Paradise: come to the fountain, and the tree of life, of the Sacred Heart of Jesus, that you may see how he has borne you in that Heart. Enter by this door into the mystical storehouse. The spouse of souls invites you there when he says: 'If any man thirst, let him come to me, and drink.'

Laurence Wartenberger

If you have any love for Our Lord, recall to mind the pains which he endured; kneel in the shadows of the Cross in contemplation; and the fruits of his bitter Passion will appear to you inestimably sweet. Am I asking anything too difficult of you when I tell you to think of him? Let not the Saviour stretch out his hands before you in vain. Seek no more unprofitable joys here below, but reserve yourself for the joys of eternity. Hear today the voice of the Lord, and harden not your heart. God asks for your heart, and he would have it humble, docile, full of goodwill and of distrust of self, and set free from every sinful affection.

7

Eighteenth and Nineteenth Centuries

Novice Master
Aula Dei Charterhouse, Spain (1758)

Emmanuel du Creux
Prior of Bourbon-les-Gaillon Charterhouse (circa 1788)

Francis de Sales Pollien
(b. 1853; d. 1936)
Member of La Torre Charterhouse, Italy

Louis-Marie Rouvier
Prior of Bosserville Charterhouse (circa 1850)

Louis-Marie Baudin
(b. 1845; d. 1926)
Prior of Montrieux Charterhouse

Novice Master, Aula Dei

Retreated into his cell, the Carthusian does not seek opportunities to mix with and indulge in dissipation with men in the outside world; he maintains his seclusion and prefers to speak to God about the needs of mankind rather than talk to laymen on divine greatness. His talk is limited to what the Rule of the Order permits and he takes care that he talks as little as possible.

Permanently united to the ancient Church's faith, a Carthusian would not even listen to an angel should the latter speak to him of false doctrines. Silence and prayer are the work of the solitary who is not devoted to preaching; he strives to offer to God fervent prayers for the peace of the Church and the conversion of those outside it, content with the insignificance of his state.

All his hopes for the present world lie within four walls during his life and in several feet under the ground after his death. In short, he aims to be free from all fear and expectations from life on earth; he rises above any earthly desires, content with hope for happiness in eternity for which he strives to prepare through continual prayer until his last breath when he presents his soul into the arms of Jesus and Mary.

Emmanuel du Creux

How glorious it is for us to be children of such a father [St Bruno]. But just to have become a member of the Order which he founded is not enough; we shall never truly be his children unless we faithfully aspire to attain his virtues. Such is the way to pay homage really to our saints – many thousand times preferable to placing their relics in gold or silver caskets decorated with precious stones . . . Wretched and weak as we are, let us try as much as possible to be deeply humble, gentle and charitable and strive to achieve the ultimate aim of our Order – union with God. To endeavour to acquire such virtues, let us retire into silence and solitude and concentrate on God . . . What more is there to want?

Tobias said to his son: 'We are children of saints.' We, too, can say the same: we enjoy the fruits of their labours; we are the heirs of their glory and goodness. Happy are we if we can attain their virtues and, if we deserve it, inherit through our faithfulness a part of the glory they have enjoyed and will enjoy throughout eternity.

Francis de Sales Pollien

The will of God follows me in all the details of my life to lead me to the supreme end of my creation. There is so much to be done in my soul that God works in it without ceasing. Thus, it is not I alone who work for the glory of God with the help of grace; it is much more God who himself works in me for his own glory, and who works in me without me, and sometimes in spite of me.

These divine operations more than anything else work to realize holiness in my soul. What I do in the way of practical piety is but little help to achieve holiness. It is not in this way that I make great progress; I am making my own very small little steps which help me forwards but little. My great progress is made when God carries me in his arms. It is the action of his good pleasure which is the principal means of my interior progress. Here, there are no longer my own little steps, but the great strides of God himself.

God alone is my strength, my support, my refuge, and my deliverance: he is my helper, my protector, my strength and my salvation. 'I am the vine,' says the Lord, 'you are the branches; he that abideth in me, and I in him, the same beareth much fruit: for without me you can do nothing' (John 15:5). He does not say: 'without me, you can do very little' but: 'without me, you can do nothing.' Without him, I can neither do little nor much. I can do nothing.

If I wish to be convinced of my impotence in detail, I have only to remind myself of what I have to do: to know, to love, to seek God as my end and his will as my way.

By my natural faculties, I can see, make decisions and act; but these things do not constitute that vision, love, and search which make up Christian piety. Piety is essentially a supernatural work, and presupposes supernatural life in the soul. The acts of this supernatural life are exercised by my natural faculties, but only by virtue of the supernatural principle which animates them. My faculties lend grace the help of their action: it is through them that grace acts, but grace is the principal agent, the essential motive, and the vital cause.

Ordinary faith suffices to cast out ordinary evil spirits, but in order to overcome more powerful adversaries, extraordinary faith is needed, and this can only be acquired by prayer and fasting. If anyone asks why prayer and fasting are essential, we must reply: man consists of body and soul, there are two substances within him, the one material and the other spiritual, and in order to resist the spirit of evil these two substances must be brought into contact with the spirit of good, and spiritualized, each in its own way. The soul is spiritualized by prayer and the body by penance, which raises it into the regions of the spirit, just as prayer uplifts the soul. Faith raises man to God, and man is too feeble to overcome evil if he lacks faith; the greater his faith the greater his strength. If he realizes his own weakness in face of the enemy, he must strive to lift himself up to God and to increase his faith, and both are done by way of prayer and penance.

Impurity triumphs everywhere, in our theatres and places of amusement, on holidays and in the streets, in pictures and books, in public institutions and even in private families. Crime of every sort abounds. The minds of all classes are being corrupted by education interwoven with falsehood, blasphemy, error and impiety. A spirit of pride and rebellion embitters individuals and stirs up the masses. Urged on by evil, men strive to enjoy pleasure in all its forms, seeking to please their bodies, hearts and minds. They wish to enjoy life, and beyond this they have no further aim, but for the sake of enjoyment they are breaking down the old barriers of respect for authority, of self-control and dignity, of uprightness and honesty, of faith and loyalty. All the old beliefs and customs, traditions and habits, even family and social life, are in danger of being swallowed up in a great cataclysm of bloodshed and sin.

To give oneself, wholly and without reserve, to God is the ideal of every religious, his impulse, his necessity, his life; and Christians recognize this fact, for we often hear it said of one who has embraced the religious life: 'He has given himself to God.' O God, raise up amongst us men capable of giving themselves to you; men capable of living for their own good and for that of your Church, men who can value their own souls and Church, and will never separate one from the other! O Lord Jesus, grant that we may become true members of your mystical body, sound and vigorous in ourselves and full of active devotion to the service of your body, the Church.

Those who see below the surface enter religion. In so doing they feel how human bonds are broken, but they are not slow to taste the sweetness of God's service. There is first a sensation of detachment, freedom and strength, which is extremely delightful. The soul perceives how mortification releases it from the tyranny of mankind; it is delivered from many forms of bondage, and no one realizes how oppressive this bondage has been until he is released from it, and his mind, heart and senses recover strength, ease, freedom and independence in a degree astonishing even to himself. His body is set free from many obligations, his heart from wearisome ties and his mind from its fetters. Well may a man desire to taste this freedom, even at the cost of some suffering.

In the second place the soul experiences the still sweeter consolation of being an instrument of atonement for the world. Generous hearts know this well, and there are few greater joys than that of bringing help to others. Does the consoler or the consoled feel the truer happiness? When a religious practises mortifications, he feels that he is doing a work of consolation and atonement; he realizes the benefit and efficacy of his sacrifices; he knows how many souls are healed, comforted and encouraged by the remedies prepared in the crucible of his sacrifice.

Life in a Carthusian monastery is full of interest and animation; uniformity and variety are so judiciously blended as to allow no scope for either exterior dissipation or interior weariness. The religious, engaged in prayer and penance, scarcely perceives the lapse of time as it passes rapidly onwards to eternity, and when at length he quits his cell for heaven, he will be far from feeling that the way thither has been tedious.

Let us once more consider Our Lord's words. He tells us that there is an abundant harvest and that the workers are few. One might fancy that he would go on to bid his apostles hasten to gather in the harvest. As the harvest is abundant and the workers are too few, the natural conclusion, at which we should arrive, would be: 'Hasten, therefore, and busy yourselves about the harvest.' But God's conclusion is: 'Pray therefore, pray the Lord of the harvest to send forth labourers into his harvest' (Matt. 9:37).

Our Lord Jesus Christ, having come into the world to do his Father's business, spent thirty years of his life in the silence of prayer and work; and during the three years that he devoted to his public ministry, he often spent whole nights in prayer to God (Luke 6:12).

His work, therefore, began with contemplation, and ended with action. The apostles, having inherited his Spirit, being trained in his school, and desiring to continue his task, at first reserved to themselves the great duty of prayer, and afterwards the ministry of the Word, delegating to others more active occupations (Acts 6:2–4), and through their prayers and words the Church received a definite organization. Around each bishop gathered a group of priests and clergy, who used to unite first in prayer before giving themselves out in action, starting from a common centre to exercise the ministry of the Church. In this way the various local churches were founded. The vital cell or nucleus at the centre of the organization was the college of priests and clergy gathered round the bishop, attending in the first place to public worship, and deriving from this prayer offered in common the strength to convert men to the faith.

Amid the religious confusion existing in our disorganized social life, may it not be of the greatest benefit to demonstrate the apostolic value of contemplation and devotion, in order that souls eager for self-sacrifice and prayer may become more numerous and more fervent?

In this matter the lead has already been admirably taken by His Holiness Pope Pius XI in that now famous Bull, *Umbratilem*, by which, in the year 1924, he approved the revised edition of the Statutes of the Carthusian Order. After referring to those solitaries who give themselves up entirely to the fulfilment of the Divine Office and to the contemplation of the divine mysteries and the eternal truths in which to the practice of both mental and bodily mortification, they join continual prayer for the extension of the kingdom of God on earth, His Holiness says that this state has always been held up by the Church for the admiration of all, since it is the most perfect form of life to which a man may be called.

He then continues: 'It is, besides, easy to understand how they who assiduously fulfil the duty of prayer and penance contribute much more to the increase of the Church and the welfare of mankind than those who labour in tilling the Master's field; for unless the former drew down from heaven a shower of divine graces to water the field that is being tilled, the evangelical labourers would reap from their toil a more scanty crop.'

The heart is set upon the one sole object of unchanging love. To love God, to grow in this love, to strive with all our might to embrace this supreme goodness and to be united to it and find all our delight in it; to practise the highest act to which man can rise, to aim at a state of pure love, the climax of our supernatural life; these are the ends towards which all our powers should converge.

We must distinguish the interior, private and personal state of a soul given up to union with God from the exterior, public and official position of an institution designed to aid contemplative vocations. The interior and personal state of contemplation is reached by a soul when its faculties and life are cut off from earth, and set upon God.

The severity of monastic penances surprises those who are not Christians; it fills cowardly souls with fear, but it attracts generous hearts. To non-Christians the idea of penance is incomprehensible; cowards understand but fear it; others both understand and love it; though these will always be in the minority.

Yet does the world offer nothing but joys to its children? Is life a rose without thorns? Alas! there are more thorns than roses, and the lamentations of those whose hearts are torn by the thorns are heard far more frequently than the joyful songs of those whose existence is crowned with roses. No, the world is not so beautiful as it seems, its yoke is sadly heavy and the burden of its labour is terribly wearisome. Knowing this, our Saviour calls us, saying: 'Come to me, all you that labour and are burdened; I will give you rest. Take my yoke upon yourselves, and learn from me; I am gentle and humble of heart; and you shall find rest for your souls. For my yoke is easy and my burden is light' (Matt. 11:28–30).

Louis-Marie Rouvier

There are great advantages to be obtained through devotion to the Blessed Virgin, and these lead us to offer all our actions through her charitable hands. Yet, there are but few souls who know this great secret of enriching themselves in time for eternity. Happy are those who put it into practice! How beautiful, rich and brilliant is the crown which awaits them in heaven!

Louis-Marie Baudin

What an example for us! Rich in the possession of her divine Son, Mary deprived herself of the goods of this world, in order to preserve her unique treasure. And yet as she was Queen of Creation, she knew that she could always have been trusted to make use of created things in a lawful and holy manner. We too, therefore, should remain detached from the vanities of this world, if we would possess him who in truth only gives himself to those who can repeat with the poor man of Assisi: 'My God, and my All!' We should conform, then, with the utmost exactitude to the provisions of our Rule which determine the scope of our vows, ever bearing in mind that forceful expression of our Statutes: 'Let the religious know that after his profession he has no longer the right to possess any object, not even the stick on which he leans to support his steps.'

'God wills', says St Bernard, 'that all his gifts should come to us through Mary.' Now, in the Carthusian life, we have four different grounds on which to thank the author of all good. We are men, Christians, religious and Carthusians. Eternity will not be long enough for us to bless that infinite goodness whose foreseeing providence is manifested in these marks of creative love, and the boundless goodness that is revealed in them.

But do we not owe something to the privileged creature through whom these divine benefits have come to us, and whose share in their distribution has been the more active and personal in proportion as the gifts are higher and more supernatural?

We must try, then, to meditate on the part assigned to Mary by almighty God in the dispensation of these gifts, and to show that our response to the advances of our gentle Mother should be one of boundless gratitude; even though, in her humility, she only seeks our thanks so that she may unite these with the ceaseless Magnificat she sings to the divine Majesty.

A certain lay-brother, Bruno Lhuillier, of the Charter-house of Bosserville, conceived a love for the Mother of God only less ardent than his devotion to her divine Son. Wherever he recognized signs of the one through whom all blessings come to the world – whether it was in the house, the garden, the woods or in the monastic enclosure – he threw himself on his knees to show his veneration and reverence for her. He never made use of any other salutation than the gentle greeting Ave Maria; and many of his brethren in religion loved to reply to him with the same words. One day, forestalled by one of them, the good brother in his joy and happiness at the sound of the familiar welcome, could only exclaim: 'Oh yes; Ave Maria! – always, always . . .'

During the first half of the last century, a Carthusian nun lay dying in the convent of Holy Cross at Beau-regard in the Dauphine in France. It had always been her delight to lavish every possible mark of her love on the Queen of virgins, above all by reciting the rosary. As she lay dying it was noticed that her eyes rested with evident joy on a certain spot from which she seemed unable to withdraw her gaze. The sisters who were attending her asked her what it was that she saw. 'Oh, do you not admire', she replied, 'that wonderful succession of rosaries which form a ladder by which I hope to reach heaven?'

This mystical ladder is within the reach of us all, and we mount a step of it every time we say with fervour: Holy Mary, Mother of God, pray for us sinners, now and at the hour of our death.

Solitude of place, of mind and of heart are of little value without solitude of soul, which consists in perfect obedience. Let us listen to our Reverend Father Dom Le Masson, writing to the nuns of the Order: 'Solitude of soul implies the cutting off of every attachment, so that the soul remains voluntarily stripped, not only of its affection, desires and cares, but even of itself. It no longer considers its own consolation, its own profit or happiness, but God alone! It is his glory that is its aim; all else is naught.'

In March of the year 1095 – that is, eleven years after the foundation of the Carthusian Order – there met at Piacenza in Lombardy one of the most important Councils of the Church held until then. It is said that St Bruno was present at it. The Acts of the Council would in that event have been the crowning of his life and devotion to the Church. The noble assembly issued a decree with regard to the adoption of the Preface of Our Lady. Many writers declare that Bruno not only inspired the decree, but himself wrote the words of the Preface, now so often repeated at the altar at the moment when in the Holy Eucharist the great mystery of the Incarnation is about to be renewed.

It is truly meet and just, right and availing unto salvation, that we should at all times and in all places give thanks unto Thee, O holy Lord, Father almighty, eternal God . . . and should praise and bless Thee and proclaim Thee in venerating the Blessed Mary, ever a virgin; who by the overshadowing of the Holy Ghost and losing not her virginity, gave forth to the world the everlasting light, Jesus Christ, our Lord.

At the Council of Piacenza, according to some writers, Bruno also expressed the desire that the Little Office of Our Lady, already recited by the monks of St Peter Damian, should be adopted by the Church, and made obligatory for all priests. This desire was not realized until the Council of Clermont some eight months later.

On her side, Our Lady treated St Bruno as a son of predilection. At the Charterhouse of La Torre in Calabria in southern Italy, it frequently happened that in the winter months our Father Bruno would at night plunge into a little lake near to the grotto where he loved to hold converse with his heavenly Mother. This icy bath lasted often for hours, especially on the eves of the greater feasts. More than once he would have died, had it not been for the miraculous intervention of Our Blessed Lady.

Devotion to Mary is thus one of the most precious legacies bequeathed to us by our founder, and we can with glad hearts attribute the numerous favours bestowed on our Order to the tender and fervent devotion of our founder to the Queen of Heaven.

It is related that when Dom Louis Rouvier was installed as Prior of the Charterhouse of Bosserville in the last century, his constant desire was to show in some way that he regarded himself in his office simply as Our Lady's vicar, and that he intended to exercise his authority solely in dependence upon her. In the church and refectory, above the Prior's seat, he placed a small statue of Our Lady bearing the inscription: 'Reign over us, O blessed Virgin, together with your Son.' At his instance also, a picture of Our Lady Immaculate was hung on all the cell doors; and in various parts of the monastery he placed prints showing Carthusians at Mary's feet offering her the homage of their love.

We, too, should never forget the tremendous honour God has paid us in allowing us to have his Mother as our Queen and to be reckoned among her servants.

8

A Twentieth-Century Carthusian Brother

Augustin Guillerand
(b. 1877; d. 1940)
Prior of Vedana Charterhouse, Italy (1935–40)

Jean-Baptiste Porion
Procurator-General of the Grande Chartreuse (1946–81)

A Twentieth-century Carthusian Prior
(b. 1933)

A Twentieth-century Carthusian
(b. 1939)

Augustin Guillerand

Has anyone ever told us what God is? No – only what he is not! In a sense, that is all one can say about him. But we must not complain; on the contrary, we should be glad for his sake, for to define anything is to set bounds to it, and God has no bounds. He is infinite. That thought ought to make us rejoice, and in all eternity it will, in fact, overwhelm us with joy. We shall be able to contemplate him unendingly, and unendingly we shall discover in him fresh perfections and beauty, and unendingly he will appear to us as unknown, as unfathomable and as desirable, as though the eye of our soul, opened wide by the light of Heaven, rested upon him for the first time.

God is. That is all he is. Every created being is something 'particular'. It is not only a being that exists, but 'such and such' a being. It has a name and form which distinguish it from everything else. Its form is constituted by its limits, by the lines which denote where it ends.

God, on the other hand, is a being of whom when one has said: 'He is', one has said it all. Having said that, one distinguishes him from everything else. Being is his form; being is his name. It is the name he gave himself, 'I am he who is.'

We are not fond of suffering, and, in one sense, we are right. We are made for happiness, and it should be the dream of our hearts, the aim of our existence. We are not wrong to seek happiness, but we are wrong to seek it along wrong paths. Where are we to find it? In God alone. He is that mysterious reality for whom we long in all that we desire, in all that we do. He hides

---

A Twentieth-Century Carthusian Brother

himself in the depths of all created things, from which we ask happiness, and which cannot give it to us. They are the veil which hides the infinite beauty of his face, and we suffer because we stop at that veil, instead of passing beyond it. When we pass beyond the veil and meet the reality which is behind it all, then we are consoled, and our joy is full.

Magnificat . . .how can one magnify God? He is infinite greatness, and one cannot add to the infinite. One cannot alter and enlarge the limits of someone who has no limits. One must not be surprised at these apparent contradictions when we speak of God. Our human language comes from something created; it is made to express things that are circumscribed. In face of the infinite, our stutterings tremble like human shoulders bent under an impossible load.

Yet Our Lady uses this vehicle which we find so inadequate. Her thought is far vaster than the words that convey it. Try hard to catch something of that immense thought.

Of all the range of colours which delight you, there remains only the long naked branches of the beech tree in the thickness of the wood . . .But your inward vision has caught and retained the essential beauty of these passing splendours, and the forest has achieved its mission in you.

Beyond finite beauty — that is, the beauty that we see — is a depth of infinite beauty from which all created beauty comes, and to which it must return to find its fulfilment. This is the light in which all works of art must be immersed, if they are to touch the depths of all being and of all hearts. God is at the deep centre of all things, and when we find him there we find eternal life. Every creature gifted with reason has received light to see in all created things both their own individual beauty and that of the Supreme Being, from whom they have received their being, and who sustains them in it. With the light given us we should see God in all things. Our gaze should pass beyond the shadows of created things in order that it may rest in the true light hidden in beings without reason, but discovered by those who have reason. And with this Being we should make ourselves in harmony.

One must contemplate the greatness of God in order to understand and experience his love; to know the Lord, the supreme Master, in order to love the Father with a love unchanging and deep, which becomes neither familiarity nor irreverence. The liveliest transports of love are born of these thoughts: this goodness so compassionate is that of the infinite Being: that love, that understanding, those exchanges of love, that life with God and in him – he alone can give them. Without him, we would possess nothing; without him we should be nothing.

At last I have found my ideal. Now I know where I want to go, where I can go, and that I shall arrive at my goal. Hitherto, I have groped my way in the darkness, the difficulties I have encountered have wearied and discouraged me. Now I know; and henceforth nothing will hold me back. I will not rest until I have found God in the innermost depths of my heart: I have found him whom my soul loveth: I hold him, and I will not let him go. Love will give me wings, for love is strong as death. Difficulties will no longer matter, for I can do all things in him who strengthens me.

If I glance over my past life and am truly sincere with myself, I will have to admit that so far my spiritual life has lacked an ideal, and that is the real reason I have made so little progress. I have failed to understand how deeply God loves and seeks souls: souls that will give themselves to him so that he may give himself to them. The degree of intimacy to which Our Lord calls us will be achieved in the measure of the generosity of our response to grace. His love is without measure, and longs to give itself completely to souls. But souls are afraid, because of the consequences of that intimacy which calls for great sacrifices on our part.

In future, however, I shall be honest with myself. On the one hand, I know that God wants to take full and entire possession of my soul and that he has predestined me to be able to conform to the image of his Son. He wants me to be his son by adoption. On the other hand, I also know that my unworthiness is no obstacle to his love. Who, indeed, could deem himself worthy? If we say that we have no sin, we deceive ourselves.

But there is much more than this. It is not in spite of our unworthiness that God seeks our love, but because of it: that he may reveal his glory in us. The more unworthy the material, the more is glory reflected on an artist who can fashion a masterpiece out of it. It is this truth that Our Lord tried to bring home to men in the parables of the prodigal son, and of the lost sheep. There is more joy in heaven, we are told, over one sinner doing penance than over all the just. If, then, I have made up my mind to persevere in my ideal, I must be continually acknowledging that, on the one hand, I am nothing and can do nothing of myself, but that, on the other hand, God is all: that he can do all things and wants to do all in me, so that I can make a complete oblation of my life to him.

By faith we adhere to the truth of the divine life offered to us. By charity this life becomes ours. By hope we are certain, with the help of grace, to live this life more and more, and finally to possess it for ever in eternity. This is the essence of all true and real prayer. Instead of frittering away our time of prayer on a variety of matters; instead of philosophizing about God, multiplying acts of the intellect, of the will and of the imagination, in order to conjure up 'pictures' of what we are thinking about, how much simpler it is to go to God directly in our hearts. Seek him in simplicity of heart. It is Our Lord himself who gives us the invitation. Be simple as doves. Man is a complex being, but it would be a pity if he introduced his complications into his relations with God. God, on

---

A Twentieth-Century Carthusian Brother

the contrary, is simplicity itself. The more complicated we are, therefore, the farther we stray from him: on the other hand, the simpler we are the closer we come to him.

We have seen that God our Father is present in us. When a child wants to talk to his father he does not make use of a manual of etiquette or a code of manners: he speaks in a simple and unaffected way, without formality; and we must do the same with our heavenly Father. He himself said: 'Unless you become as little children, you shall not enter into the kingdom of heaven.' A mother never grows tired of hearing her little one say: 'Mother, I love you.' It is the same with God. The more childlike our prayer, the more it is pleasing to him. After all it was he who chose for himself the name of Father. It is the Holy Spirit who cries in us: Abba, Pater. It is the Holy Spirit also who places on our lips the inspired words of Scripture and of other liturgical texts.

Our prayer, then, must be quite simple – as simple as possible. All we have to do is to place ourselves on our knees, and with complete sincerity make our acts of faith, hope and love. There is no method of prayer more certain, more elevated and more salutary than this.

A Twentieth-century Carthusian Prior

The starting-point of our silence can only be God himself who calls; to want to establish recollection from our own resources would be to plunge into a foolish adventure. 'He alone who listens in silence hears the whisper of the gentle breeze that reveals the presence of the Lord.' From the moment we realize the Lord is inviting us to follow him in that direction, we should make ourselves available, but, like Elijah on the summit of Horeb, it is neither in the wind nor in the earthquake nor in the fire that we will find silence. The latter will come upon us when it is born of God himself in the form of a gentle breeze.

Silence is the work of God; but, it is much more than that, as we said: it is God's word. There lies the ultimate root of the humility which must become our very element if we wish to discover the source of silence in our heart.

To 'make' prayer. The expression is strange since it suggests the idea of doing something, of obtaining a result, of producing or creating. There, one finds again the old temptation of Western contemplative thinking symbolized in the juggler of Notre Dame. The story is touching in so far as it shows us that God hardly pays attention to what one does for him, since he sees the heart and not the deeds. Therefore, it is sad to see that the poor juggler little realized that it was enough to let his heart rest in the presence of the Lord in order to give him the very best. He had to do his juggling. It was not Our Lady who needed to see him dance, it was the juggler himself who needed to do something. It was for him a matter of 'making' prayer.

It is not a question of 'making' prayer or even of making silence. Silence is not contrived. When one comes before the Lord with the mind full of images, with strong emotions and one's thoughts still in movement, one realizes the need for silence, the temptation then is to make silence. As if it were a question of clothing oneself in silence, of throwing over all the inner murmurings a cape which would hide or smother it. This is not to be silent, it is rather to cover up the noise or shut it up within ourselves, so that it is always ready to emerge at the slightest opportunity. There is no need to create silence or to inject it from without. It is already there and it is simply a matter of letting it rise from within us so that it eliminates by its very presence the noise that distracts or invades us. Silence can be mere nothingness: silence of the stone, the silence of the mind numbed and deadened by its involvement with the material and exterior. This is not true silence. The only silence that counts is the presence of him who is nothing.

Does not prayer often mean returning gradually and simply to true silence? Certainly, not by doing anything or imposing some kind of yoke or burden on ourselves but, on the contrary, by letting all our activity subside, little by little, into that true interior silence that will begin to assert itself and resume its rightful place. Once we have heard this silence we thirst to find it again. We must, however, free ourselves from the idea that we can of ourselves reproduce it. It is there; it is always there even if we no longer hear it. Indeed, there are days when it is impossible to recapture it, for the mill of the mind is grinding and it is impossible to stop the workings of the imagination and the senses. Yet, silence does abide in the depths of our will as a peaceful and tranquil acceptance of the noise and disturbances that hinder our coming to serenity of mind. Normally, though, it should be possible by means of a certain physical and intellectual asceticism (breathing, posture, etc.) to calm the undisciplined impulses of the mind in order to achieve at least a little stillness. All the same, silence is more profound than all accepted forms of meditation: lectio divina, lights from the Lord that help us penetrate his mysteries, reflection on themes that merit our attention, etc. All this is good and helps us to approach the truth. It is all very necessary in its own time.

When I pray, I do not call on the God of philosophers nor even, in a sense, on the God of theologians. I turn to my Father or rather, our Father. To be more precise, I turn to him whom Jesus, in complete intimacy and confidence, called Abba. When the disciples asked our Lord to teach them how to pray, he simply replied: 'When you pray you say: "Abba" . . .' To name God thus is to have the certainty that we are loved; a certitude of a different nature from that referred to by scholars but one derived from innermost conviction; a certitude of faith at which we have arrived, it seems to us, after periods of reflection, meditation and consideration of our interior inspirations; though ultimately this certitude is a gift. We have complete faith in the love we have in our hearts because it is the Father who has sent us his Spirit, now that his Son has entered into his glory.

It is because the Father loves me that I am able to turn

to him in complete trust and confidence. I do not turn toward him to stress my virtues, nor for well-calculated reasons, but trusting in the infinite tenderness of the Abba for his Son Jesus, since he is also my Abba.

Contemplation is a participation in divine life, in the knowledge and love of God. Christian contemplation is the awakening of the life of Christ in us through the breath of the Spirit: his gaze on the Father, his love for mankind. Our prayer is a bringing to the fore of the grace of Christ by which, as members of Christ's body, sons in the Son, we enter into the life of the Trinity: the exchange of love among the Father, the Son and the Holy Spirit.

The Father is the source of everything; through love he gives everything to the Son. His joy is in giving, in giving his very self: total fruitfulness, eternal poverty, because he keeps nothing back for himself. The Father sends himself forth totally in his unique Word.

The Son receives everything from the Father, eternally. To be the Son is always to be turned towards the Father so as to receive everything from him, and by the power of this received life, to give everything back to the Father in a rebounding of love and gratitude.

This outpouring, the link which unites the Father and the Son in a reciprocal gift of love, is the Holy Spirit, poverty twice over, born of the gift, in the gift, for the gift. Divine love only exists as giving itself, as losing itself completely and eternally.

Since God is love, the life of the Trinity is seen as the unconditional gift of reciprocal love. In the Three Persons, the divine nature exists precisely as given. Who can be poorer than God? He alone knows how to give himself completely. And precisely by this 'GiftLove' he is fulfilled. This law is seen to be verified in the incarnation of the Son.

A Twentieth-century Carthusian Brother

Silence
Silent in the face of beauty
Silent in the morning light
Silent on the way of duty
Silent in the awesome night

Silent on the way to silence
Where the Word unspoken dwells
Silent on the way to silence
Where the longed-for Jesus dwells